Hercules

by Nancy Loewen

Consultant:
Kenneth F. Kitchell Jr., Ph.D.
Department of Classics
University of Massachusetts, Amherst

RiverFront Books

an imprint of Franklin Watts
A Division of Grolier Publishing
New York   London   Hong Kong   Sydney
Danbury, Connecticut

RiverFront Books
http://publishing.grolier.com

Library of Congress Cataloging-in-Publication Data
Loewen, Nancy, 1964–
    Hercules/by Nancy Loewen.
    p. cm.—(Greek and Roman mythology)
    Includes bibliographical references and index.
    Summary: Surveys classical mythology, discussing the relationship between
Greek and Roman myths, and describes the birth and life of the demigod Hercules,
known as Heracles in Greek mythology.
    ISBN 0-7368-0049-2
    1. Hercules (Roman mythology)—Juvenile literature. [1. Hercules (Roman
mythology) 2. Heracles (Greek mythology) 3. Mythology, Roman. 4. Mythology,
Greek.] I. Title. II. Series.
BL820.H5L64   1999
292.2'113—dc21
                                                                    98-35118
                                                                         CIP
                                                                          AC

Editorial Credits

Christy Steele, editor; Clay Schotzko/Icon Productions, cover designer;
    Timothy Halldin, illustrator; Sheri Gosewisch, photo researcher

Photo credits

Archive Photos, 6, 17, 27, 33
Art Resource, cover, 14; Erich Lessing, 4, 18, 21, 34, 36; Scala, 25, 28, 31, 38
Unicorn Stock Photos/Jean Higgins, 22
Visuals Unlimited/Audrey Gibson, 40
William B. Folsom, 11

Table of Contents

This book is illustrated with photographs of statues, paintings, illustrations, and other artwork about mythology by artists from both ancient and modern times.

Chapter One

About Mythology

Ancient Greek and Roman communities existed as long ago as 2000 B.C. People living in these communities used stories to help them understand the world.

Ancient Greeks and Romans believed that their stories were true. In the stories, gods, goddesses, heroes, and monsters controlled the earth. Most ancient people did not know much about science. So stories about these characters explained human history and the natural world. The stories created a sense of order and understanding in their lives.

People today call stories like these myths because no one believes in the stories any longer. A myth is a story with a purpose. Classical mythology is the collection of the hundreds of Greek and Roman myths.

Ancient Greek and Roman communities existed as long ago as 2000 B.C. Ruins from these communities still stand today.

Explanation myths explain natural events such as the groupings of stars in the sky.

There are two kinds of Greek and Roman myths. Each type of myth has a certain purpose. Explanation myths explain natural events such as the groupings of stars in the sky.

Quest myths describe a character's search for something. The search may be for treasure or for a person. Heroes usually are the main characters in quest myths. Heroes must face dangers and hardships to complete their quests. They succeed because they are brave, smart, or strong. Quest myths teach people to keep trying to accomplish their goals even during hard times. A hero named Hercules appears in many quest myths.

History of Classical Mythology
People do not believe the stories from classical mythology anymore. Instead, science helps us explain why things happen in nature.

The myths in classical mythology started in both ancient Greece and Rome. Greece is a country in what is now Europe. The Roman Empire was a group of countries under Roman rule. Rome was the capital city of the Roman Empire. Rome is now in Italy.

Greek people were among the first people to tell myths. They developed myths about gods, goddesses, heroes, and monsters in about 2000 B.C.

The Roman Empire conquered Greece around 100 B.C. The Roman government ruled Greece. Roman people liked the Greek myths. They began telling stories about characters from Greek myths. The Romans gave their characters different names. This book uses the Roman names of the characters.

Gods and Goddesses
of Greek and Roman Mythology

Zeus (Greek)   Jupiter (Roman)
King of the gods and goddesses

Hera (Greek)   Juno (Roman)
Queen of the gods and goddesses

Athena (Greek)   Minerva (Roman)
Goddess of wisdom and war

Apollo (Greek)   No Roman Name
God of beauty, the Sun, prophecy, and healing

Artemis (Greek)   Diana (Roman)
Goddess of the moon and the hunt

Hermes (Greek)   Mercury (Roman)
God of business and commerce; messenger to Zeus

Aphrodite (Greek)   Venus (Roman)
Goddess of love, beauty, and fertility

Dionysus (Greek)   Bacchus (Roman)
God of wine, song, and drama

Poseidon (Greek)   Neptune (Roman)
God of the seas

Hades (Greek)   Pluto (Roman)
God of the Underworld

Demeter (Greek)   Ceres (Roman)
Goddess of agriculture

Ares (Greek)   Mars (Roman)
God of war

Hephaestus (Greek)   Vulcan (Roman)
God of fire

Hestia (Greek)   Vesta (Roman)
Goddess of the hearth

Many people who lived in ancient Greece and the Roman Empire did not know how to write and read. Instead, storytellers memorized myths and told the stories to the people. The storytellers sometimes added new ideas to make the myths seem more exciting. Many versions of the myths exist today because storytellers told the myths in different ways.

History of the Gods
Earth and Heaven were the oldest gods. They had many children. They had 150-handed giants, powerful giants called titans, and cyclopes. Cyclopes were one-eyed giants.

The titan Cronus did not like how his father ruled the world. So Cronus conquered Heaven and became the ruler. Cronus married his sister Rhea. They had six children. Cronus did not want his children to conquer him. So he ate all of them but one. Rhea hid Jupiter from Cronus.

Jupiter grew up. Another titan gave Jupiter a special potion to help him free his brothers and sisters. Jupiter disguised himself and gave the drink to Cronus. The potion made Jupiter's brothers and sisters come out of Cronus' body.

Cronus' children combined forces to fight their father. Finally, they won. Jupiter locked Cronus underground.

Jupiter ruled over his brothers and sisters on Mount Olympus. Some of them married each other and had children. These Olympian gods are the main characters in classical mythology.

Gods and Goddesses

Some gods and goddesses were more powerful than others. Myths often tell about these powerful beings fighting amongst themselves to increase their power and rank. People believed the most powerful gods and goddesses lived on top of Mount Olympus. This is the highest mountain in Greece. Less important gods and goddesses lived throughout the earth, sky, and sea.

The gods and goddesses behaved very much like humans. They could be envious, greedy, or mean. They also could be loving, faithful, and brave. But unlike humans, the gods had magical powers that were almost unlimited. They could change themselves or humans into different

People believed the powerful gods and goddesses lived on top of Mount Olympus.

shapes. They could create objects, storms, monsters, or people. Most importantly, the gods and goddesses were immortal. They did not die.

Religion

Greeks and Romans worshiped the gods and goddesses in their stories. These powerful beings were the focus of Greek and Roman religion.

Each person chose which god or goddess to worship. They worshiped the powerful beings that mattered most to their lives. Soldiers might worship Mars. He is the god of war. Hunters might pray to Diana. She is goddess of the hunt.

Greeks and Romans honored the gods and goddesses in many ways. Some built temples to honor their favorite gods or goddesses.

People brought offerings of money and food to the temples. Some Greek and Roman citizens became priests or priestesses in the temples. They served the god or goddess of the temples by praying and performing ceremonies. Other people became artists. Artists painted pictures and made statues of the gods and goddesses. Some of the artwork decorated the temples.

Characters in Mythology

Classical mythology contained hundreds of characters. Some characters appeared in many different stories. Others were in only a few stories. Most characters belonged to one of the following groups:

Titans: These gods and goddesses were powerful giants. They were the children of Earth and Heaven.

Olympians: These were the main gods in classical mythology. Olympians looked like humans. But they had magic powers. They ruled from the top of Mount Olympus. Jupiter was the head of the Olympians.

Lesser gods: These gods were less powerful than the Olympians. They often were associated with one particular area such as a river or mountain.

Demigods: These characters were half god and half human. They had more power than ordinary humans, but were weaker than the gods. Demigods were not immortal.

Monsters: Monsters could be a combination of different animals or of animals and humans. Gods sent monsters to punish people.

Chapter Two

Hercules the Demigod

Greeks and Romans told many stories about the hero Hercules. Hercules is the Roman name for the hero. Heracles was his Greek name.

Hercules was the most famous demigod. As a demigod, he was half god and half human. Jupiter was Hercules' father. His mother was a mortal woman named Alcmene. Hercules had superhuman strength because he was a demigod. He was brave too. Hercules' hands were deadly weapons. He used them to kill many monsters.

It is likely that the myths about Hercules were based on a real person whose accomplishments became exaggerated as time passed. Or the myths might have been based on the lives of several people. But through myths,

Hercules was the most famous demigod.

Hercules became one of the world's first superheroes.

Birth of Hercules

Jupiter married an envious goddess named Juno. But Jupiter still had relationships with women on Earth. Jupiter liked a beautiful woman named Alcmene. But Alcmene refused Jupiter's advances. She wanted to remain faithful to her husband. One night, Jupiter used his powers to make himself look like Alcmene's husband. Later, Alcmene discovered that she was pregnant. She gave birth to Hercules nine months later.

Alcmene realized that her child was different from other children. Even as a baby, Hercules had incredible strength.

Amazing Strength

Juno was angry with Jupiter for having a child with Alcmene. Juno decided to punish Jupiter by killing Hercules. She put two huge snakes into Hercules' crib when he was eight months old. Hercules grabbed the snakes' necks and squeezed their throats until they died.

Hercules grabbed the snakes' necks and squeezed their throats until they died.

Alcmene raised Hercules as if he were a mortal child. Hercules went to school and learned to read and write. He also learned to play musical instruments.

Hercules' powers became greater as he grew older. But he did not learn how to control his strength or his temper. One day, Hercules went to a music lesson. He became angry with his teacher and hit the teacher on the head with a lyre. A lyre is a small, harp-like instrument. Hercules hit the teacher too hard. The teacher

died. Hercules did not mean to kill his teacher.
But he could not control himself.

In the Mountains

Alcmene felt that Hercules was too dangerous
to be around people. She sent Hercules to live
in the mountains. He took care of his family's
cattle, which grazed in mountain pastures.

Hercules' strength was useful in the
mountains. He killed many dangerous beasts
that lived there. Hercules was 18 years old
when he killed a fierce lion with his bare hands.
The lion had attacked people and cattle in the
area for years.

The Marriage of Hercules

The king of the city of Thebes was grateful
to Hercules for killing the lion. The king
thanked Hercules for his help by arranging for
Hercules to marry Princess Megara.

Hercules fell in love with the king's
daughter. He and Megara married. Megara gave
birth to several sons. The family enjoyed a
happy life.

Hercules was 18 years old when he killed a fierce lion
with his bare hands.

But Juno still wanted to hurt Hercules. She planned a way to seek revenge and rob Hercules of his happiness.

Juno used her power to make Hercules become crazy. Under Juno's power, Hercules thought his family members were dangerous snakes. He killed the snakes. Juno then let Hercules regain his senses. Hercules realized that he had killed his wife and sons by mistake.

Hercules missed his family. He felt guilty and sorry for his horrible mistake. He wanted to find a way to stop feeling guilty.

Hercules felt guilty and sorry for his horrible mistake.

Chapter Three

The 12 Labors of Hercules

Hercules traveled to the Oracle of Delphi for advice. Ancient Greeks and Romans believed gods and goddesses spoke to them through oracles. Oracles were priests or priestesses.

The oracle told Hercules to serve his cousin, King Eurystheus. Hercules had to perform whatever task King Eurystheus set for him for 10 years. The gods and goddesses would forgive Hercules for killing his family after 10 years. They also promised to take away Hercules' guilt.

Juno was pleased with the oracle's decision. King Eurystheus was a mean man who disliked Hercules. Juno knew that King Eurystheus would give Hercules difficult and dangerous

Hercules traveled to the Oracle of Delphi for advice. This photograph shows the ruins of the temple at Delphi.

tests. These tests became known as the 12 labors of Hercules.

The Lion of Nemea

King Eurystheus ordered Hercules to kill the lion of Nemea. This lion was a monster with supernatural strength. No weapon could pass through its thick skin. King Eurystheus believed the lion would kill Hercules.

Hercules found the lion. He beat it with a club to make it tired. He then wrapped his strong hands around the lion's throat and squeezed until the lion died.

Hercules used the lion's claws to cut off its pelt. A pelt is an animal's skin with the hair or fur still on it. From then on, Hercules wore the lion's thick pelt around his shoulders. It showed people how strong he was. The pelt also protected him from weapons.

The Lernean Hydra

Next, King Eurystheus told Hercules to kill the Lernean hydra. The hydra was a nine-headed monster that lived in a swamp. Its breath and blood were poisonous.

Hercules killed the Nemean lion.

Hercules asked his nephew Iolaus to help. They traveled to the swamp. Hercules filled his lungs with fresh air and ran to fight the hydra. He tried to cut off some of the hydra's heads with his sword. Two heads grew to replace every head Hercules chopped off.

Finally, Hercules had an idea. He cut off one of the hydra's heads. He asked Iolaus to sear the bloody stump before the new heads could grow. Sear means to seal with strong heat. No heads grew once Iolaus seared the wound. Hercules chopped off the other heads and Iolaus seared the wounds.

The hydra's ninth head was immortal. Hercules buried the head under a huge boulder. The hydra's head was still alive. But it could do no more harm.

Other Labors

Hercules' abilities upset King Eurystheus. The king wanted Hercules to fail. So he found even harder tasks for Hercules to do.

The king ordered Hercules to capture goddess Diana's hind of Cyreneia. The hind was a rare white deer with golden horns. Diana might kill someone she caught trying to capture her deer.

The Cyreneian hind was very quick. She ran away from Hercules whenever he came close to her. Hercules chased the hind for about one year. He finally captured the hind with a net and brought it to the king.

Next, the king told Hercules to bring back a wild boar. The king told Hercules to bring back the boar healthy and alive. Hercules trapped the boar with a net and brought it to the king.

Hercules chopped off the hydra's heads and Iolaus seared the wounds.

The next task was unpleasant. King Eurystheus told Hercules to clean King Augeas' stables in just one day. No one had ever cleaned the stables. More than 3,000 cows lived in the stables. Huge piles of dung littered the ground. People could smell the stables from great distances.

Hercules captured the mad Cretan bull.

Hercules cleaned the stables without ever touching the dung. He built a dam to change the course of a nearby river. The river's new route then flowed through the stables and washed them clean.

During the next three labors, Hercules drove away a flock of man-eating Stymphalian birds. He captured and brought back the mad Cretan bull. Hercules tamed the man-eating horses of Diomedes for his eighth labor.

The Amazon Queen

Hercules became more famous every time he completed a test. King Eurystheus became angrier every time Hercules completed a test.

The king thought for a long time before giving Hercules his next labor. Eurystheus wanted to find something very difficult for Hercules to do. So the king commanded Hercules to bring back the jeweled belt of the Amazon queen. The Amazon queen was the powerful leader of a tribe of warrior women.

At first, this task seemed as though it would be the easiest of all. The Amazon queen liked Hercules. She took off the belt and gave it to him. But then Juno interfered. She made herself look like an Amazon warrior. Juno then told the other Amazons that Hercules had come to kill the Amazon queen.

The Amazons attacked Hercules to protect their queen. Hercules believed that the queen had tricked him. He killed the Amazon queen and took her belt. He fought the Amazons and won. He then went back and gave the belt to King Eurystheus.

Geryon

Next, King Eurystheus ordered Hercules to bring back Geryon's famous red cows. Geryon was a giant with three bodies above his waist. He lived on a distant island.

Hercules sailed to the island. He began loading the cows onto his ship. Geryon heard Hercules and came to protect his cows. Hercules shot one poisoned arrow into each of Geryon's three bodies. Geryon died. Hercules sailed back to King Eurystheus with the cattle.

Golden Apples of the Hesperides

Hercules' next task was difficult. The king wanted him to bring back the golden apples of the Hesperides. The Hesperides were the daughters of a titan named Atlas. They watched over the special tree on which the apples grew. A dragon with 100 heads also guarded the tree.

Hercules did not want to fight the dragon. Instead, he asked Atlas to get the apples. Atlas

Atlas was in charge of holding the heavens.

was in charge of holding the heavens on his
shoulders. Atlas agreed to get the apples from
his daughters. But Atlas needed Hercules to hold
up the heavens until he returned with the apples.
Hercules agreed.

Atlas soon came back with the golden apples.
But he did not want to carry the heavens
anymore. He decided to leave Hercules in charge.

Hercules was mad that Atlas had tricked him.
He decided to trick Atlas too. Hercules asked

Atlas to hold the heavens for one minute so he could get into a comfortable position. Atlas took the heavens back on his shoulders. Hercules immediately ran away with the apples.

Cerberus

King Eurystheus picked the most horrible and challenging task for the 12th labor. The king told Hercules to bring Cerberus back to him. Cerberus was a fierce, three-headed dog that belonged to Pluto, the god of the Underworld. The Underworld was the home of the dead. Pluto made Cerberus guard the gates of the Underworld.

Hercules traveled to the Underworld. He asked Pluto whether he could take Cerberus to King Eurystheus. Pluto gave Hercules permission. But he would not let Hercules use weapons. He did not want Cerberus to be hurt.

Cerberus attacked Hercules. Hercules squeezed the dog's neck so hard that he almost strangled it. This kept the dog under control. Hercules then dragged the growling Cerberus to the king's palace.

Hercules traveled to the Underworld to get Cerberus.

The king was terrified. He promised
Hercules that his labors would be over if he
would return Cerberus to Pluto. Hercules
brought the dog back to the Underworld.

The gods forgave Hercules for killing his
family. They took away his terrible guilt.
Hercules' 12 labors made him a famous hero.

Chapter Four

Hercules' Later Years

Hercules had many adventures after he finished his 12 labors. He rescued people from monsters. He traveled to distant places and did good deeds.

Hercules also joined different armies and fought for good causes. He punished people who broke laws and rulers who made bad laws.

Deianira and Nessus

Hercules eventually married again. Deianira was his new wife. One day, Hercules and Deianira were traveling. They had to cross a wide river.

A centaur named Nessus lived by the river. A centaur was half man and half horse. Hercules paid Nessus to carry his wife across the river.

Hercules paid Nessus to carry his wife across the river.

Hercules became immortal.

Hercules then swam across the river and waited for them on the other side.

Nessus attacked Deianira. Hercules heard Deianira scream. He swam back across the river and shot Nessus with a poisoned arrow.

Nessus told Deianira that his blood was a love potion that would make Hercules love her forever. Deianira believed Nessus. She put some of Nessus' blood in a special bottle. She saved it to use if Hercules fell in love with someone else.

Hercules Becomes a God

Hercules was not faithful to Deianira. Deianira feared that she was losing Hercules' love. She wanted to make Hercules love her again.

Deianira smeared Nessus' blood on Hercules' clothes. But this was a trick. Nessus' blood was poisonous. Hercules put on his clothes and became sick as soon as Nessus' blood touched his skin. Deianira killed herself when she realized what she had done.

Hercules was in great pain. He knew he would slowly become sicker until he died from the poison. He did not want to suffer anymore.

Hercules had people build his funeral pyre. A pyre is a pile of wood and branches built to burn a dead body for a funeral. Hercules lay down on the pyre. He ordered people to light the fire.

But Hercules did not die. Fire and lightning rushed down from the sky just as the pyre began burning. The fire and lightning were really Jupiter. He carried Hercules to Mount Olympus in his chariot. Jupiter made Hercules a god. Hercules became immortal.

Chapter Five

Mythology in the Modern World

Characters from Greek and Roman myths have affected many areas of modern life. Hercules is especially well known. He is the hero of many popular movies, cartoons, comic books, and television programs.

Hercules' name has even become a part of the English language. Herculean means having unusually great strength. Herculean also means an unusually hard challenge. For example, someone might work very hard to complete a challenging task. This person would be making a Herculean effort to finish the task. A person might compare a hard assignment at school with the 12 labors of Hercules.

Hercules is an especially well-known character from classical mythology.

People often create buildings that look like ancient
Greek or Roman temples.

Art, Architecture, and Literature
Characters in mythology are central figures in
many famous paintings and sculptures. Pictures
of heroes, gods, goddesses, and monsters
decorate ancient vases and jars.

Myths have influenced architecture.
Architecture is the planning of buildings.
People often create buildings that look like
ancient Greek or Roman temples. These modern

40

buildings may have many columns like the temples once had.

Myths have influenced books and stories. Famous books and stories often refer to characters or actions from myths. Many heroes from popular books are similar to Hercules. People today still enjoy reading the myths themselves. Students often study myths about Hercules in school.

Geographical Names

People sometimes named geographical features after characters in classical mythology. Ancient Greeks and Romans named some places after Hercules. Columns of rock on each side of the Strait of Gibraltar are called the Pillars of Hercules. The Strait of Gibraltar is a narrow passage of water between Europe and Africa.

Ancient Greeks and Romans told a story to explain the creation of the strait. A mountain range got in Hercules' way while he was sailing to Geryon's island. Hercules moved the mountains apart so he could sail between them. This formed the strait.

Ancient Greece and Rome

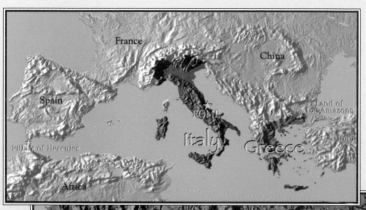

A Roman myth also explains how Earth's galaxy received its name. Jupiter brought Hercules to Mount Olympus when he was an infant. He put Hercules to Juno's breast to nurse while Juno was sleeping. Juno soon woke up. She angrily pulled Hercules away from her breast. Her milk sprayed into the heavens and formed the Milky Way galaxy.

The Test of Time
The world has changed since the days when ancient Greeks and Romans told myths to explain the world. Today, most people do not worship the gods and goddesses in mythology. People rarely tell new myths to explain the world. Instead, most people trust scientists to explain the principles of nature.

But people still enjoy reading classical mythology. Adventure, love, magic, and surprise fill the pages of myths. The stories connect people today with people from another time. They help today's readers understand the feelings, hopes, and dreams of people who lived thousands of years ago.

Words to Know

Amazon (A-muh-zahn)—a member of a tribe of warrior women

centaur (SEN-tor)—a creature with the head and chest of a human and the body of a horse

cyclops (SYE-clahpss)—a giant with one eye in the middle of its forehead

demigod (DE-mee-gahd)—a half-human, half-god character in mythology

immortal (i-MOR-tuhl)—having the ability to live forever

myth (MITH)—a story with a purpose; myths often describe quests or explain natural events.

oracle (OR-uh-kuhl)—a Greek or Roman priest or priestess through whom the gods spoke

pelt (PELT)—an animal's skin with the hair or fur still on it

pyre (PYER)—a pile of wood built to burn a dead body for a funeral

sear (SIHR)—to seal with strong heat

titan (TYE-tuhn)—a powerful giant

To Learn More

Evslin, Bernard. *The Nemean Lion.* Broomall,
Penn.: Chelsea House, 1990.

Geringer, Laura. *Hercules the Strong Man.*
New York: Scholastic, 1996.

Green, Robert Lancelyn. *Tales of the Greek
Heroes.* New York: Puffin, 1995.

Lasky, Kathryn. *Hercules: The Man, the Myth,
the Hero.* New York: Hyperion Books for
Children, 1997.

Useful Addresses

American Classical League
Miami University
Oxford, OH 45056-1694

American Philological Association
19 University Place, Room 328
New York, NY 10003-4556

**Classical Association of the Middle West
and South**
Department of Classics
Randolph-Macon College
Ashland, VA 23005

Ontario Classical Association
2072 Madden Boulevard
Oakville, ON L6H 3L6
Canada

Internet Sites

The Book of Gods, Goddesses, Heroes, and Other Characters of Mythology
http://www.cybercomm.net/~grandpa/gdsindex.html

Encyclopedia Mythica
http://www.pantheon.org/mythica/areas

Mythology
http://www.windows.umich.edu/mythology/mythology.html

Myths and Legends
http://pubpages.unh.edu/~cbsiren/myth.html

The Perseus Project
http://www.perseus.tufts.edu/

World Mythology: Ancient Greek and Roman
http://www.artsMIA.org/mythology/ancientgreekandroman.html

Index